Getting the Life
of an
Instructional Designer

By Beverly A. Reynolds

Contents

Welcome 3

What is your motivation? 3

Education 5

Finding a Job 19

Using Social Media 23

Qualities of Great Training 28

Training Deliverables 32

A Day in the Life 35

Working for Yourself 38

Summary 40

Welcome

Congratulations on taking your first step towards YOUR professional success!

In the pages of this book, we will cover the following topics:

- *Education*
- *Finding a Job*
- *Using Social Media*
- *Qualities of Great Training*
- *Training Deliverables*
- *A Day in the Life*
- *Working for Yourself*

So at that, let's get started learning.

What is your motivation?

Playing to your Strengths

The first thing to talk about is your motivation to getting into Instructional Design. Knowing your motivation will steer your career in a specific direction based on your interests. If you are good at modifying graphics, images or logos, then there is a good chance that a graphical-related profession, such as Graphic Design at an agency might just be the place for you.

On the other hand, if you are good at writing step-by-step procedures and have a passion for working with some sort of customer base, then Instructional Design may be the best bet for you.

Finally, if you are good at managing projects and timelines, then a Training Manager job is what you may be better suited.

Emulate Success

If you once knew an Instructional Designer, your motivation would be to emulate what they did that was successful and to think about how you would have handled their challenges in a more successful way.

Perhaps there was a person in your recent past that had the title of Instructional Designer and you were a stand-up Corporate Instructor. Maybe you liked the independence that the Instructional Designer had over you, but you thought you might miss the people interactions of your job is you changed positions. You might be surprised that as YOU become an Instructional Designer, you might find the best of both worlds.

Perhaps Instructional Design is something that interests you because it aligns with your talents. For instance, a job you love is a job you are more than likely going to stick with long-term. Said differently, if you are good at working with layers of an image in Photoshop, then you might work well in a fast-passed ad agency with quick graphical turnarounds. Likewise, if a job is busy, it is less likely to cause you stress if you enjoy the work, the people or something about it brings you joy. The same is true when you are valued or feel you may be making a difference.

No matter your motivation, the content of this book will assist you in making <u>YOUR</u> next steps.

Definition and Terms

The term Instructional Design encompasses many, many terms. Ultimately, Instructional Design refers to the method or way that one uses to teach one or more people – regardless of the tool or media.

In today's day and age, students are reached in different ways – often a vast variety of ways, in fact. When students are polled as to how they are best reached for maximum understanding, multi-media is often a common theme, regardless of the age of the learner. Terms such as student, learner, or even adult learning, are used interchangeably.

In order to bring students alongside you, the students must feel they are an equal to you and that the playing field is even. The job of an educator is to teach, not to manage. Sometimes this can be accomplished by visualizing yourself in the shoes of the average student – or a specific student. That is, pretend you are sitting in their chair and having to learn from <u>YOU</u>. You might be asking how you can do this when you are not physically anyone but the instructor, but if you cater the training based on their feedback – both good and bad – then they will feel as if they are a part of the classroom.

If you were to teach a more complex concept, find a way to related it back to their life. Get students to trust you as the instructor.

If you want to convey a specific message, find ways for your students to commit the content to memory. For instance, use acronyms that are fun and memorable. Find graphical ways for your students to remember a topic, even if it makes them laugh when they think about what they learned from you. *For example, if you want them to learn about a famous cook, try associating the content with a smell in your classroom.*

Finally, if you want students to retain and not just memorize, consider putting the content into practice. Include learning exercises into your training, regardless of whether learning is taking place in a classroom or over an intranet or the internet. Sometimes the use of a visual, chart, multimedia or a variety in style is just enough to have students <u>STOP</u> and pause. These tools can cause a physical break in the content for student learners to actually absorb the details.

Let's look at the Education needed to become an Instructional Designer.

Education

Keep in mind that one of the best ways to educate is through storytelling.

My Bachelor's degree is in Graphic Design and Studio Arts; however, not everything can be learned in a classroom. My first Instructional Design job was for a hospitality company. They hired me from a software test lab. At the time, I was testing software and sending the bugs to developers with step-by-step instruction.

The Training Team saw that I was doing this and thought I would be a great addition to their team. So I joined the team and learned Adobe® *RoboHelp*, *RoboDemo* (at the time), and eventually, Adobe® *Captivate*. I was given an opportunity because someone noticed I had a desired skillset or ability, at a younger age, to place an order to content, recognize pathing and articulate the detailed information with ease.

The moral of this story is that you never know where your life can go. Life often takes many turns. If you had asked me in college, or even high school, if I would really enjoy writing books or courses for a living, I am not sure what I would have told you in response. Focus on what you are good at and capitalize on those skills. Sometimes your next position will be spun off something you already know.

We will now detail the Areas of Education.

Areas of Education

At the beginning of this book, we listed the topics starting with Education. Whether you are starting a new career or increasing your knowledge as an Instructional Designer, it is important to become educated. Once you educate yourself, it is essential that you do not stop there – never stop learning. Technology changes, as do the trending methodologies on which training is built. It is also possible that specific industries as a whole will have certain rules and requirements.

Within Education, we will focus in on four main topics:

What are the <u>tools</u> available for each type of training?

There will be a need to often learn a new software package. This could take a little bit of research on your behalf. Each tool can help or aid you in doing something very specific.

What are the types of <u>resources</u> available?

Sometimes people decide on a new career, but are unclear how to actually make the jump. Did you know that there are both <u>FREE</u> and paid resources to help to take that next leap?

What are some training and development <u>theories</u> companies may employ?

This book helps you talk to a recruiter or hiring manager by equipping you with key terms. These will not just help you get the job, but also help you know what step to take next when you actually land your dream job.

What is the <u>timing</u> of training?

That is, what is the best time to take training – is it while employed or unemployed? You have to know what works best for <u>YOUR</u> situation.

We will begin with the Tools of training.

Tools

There are several tools used in this industry!

The word 'tools' is really more than just software packages, but this is where we will begin. It is simply not enough to learn a new software program.

You may also need to know how to tune audio using a microphone, run a video camera, edit video presentations, learn how to install and use *Webex®* and maybe even how to use an electronic board or projection system.

Each Instructional Design tool is meant to serve a different and unique function. If you are going to create a software simulation, you will probably not use *Adobe® Illustrator* to have the mouse move. Instead, you might learn and create your simulation with an application, such as *Adobe® Captivate*.

Each software package comes with a different learning curve. *For example, you might find it easier to learn Microsoft® Word than Adobe® Flash due to the scenes and stage.*

It is a great idea to seek out what employers are looking for in terms of software knowledge.

Software

The tools and software packages mentioned in this book are only meant as examples, and are by no means an endorsement for inclusion or exclusion. There is a software package available for every type of training deliverable. You <u>MUST</u> know what tools can produce each type of result and the capabilities of the software. *For example, if you are working for a client and they have asked you to create a transparent GIF, Adobe® RoboHelp, being a help system solution, will not aid you in graphic creation of any type.*

As with anything in life, there are multiple ways or multiple software packages that will often get the job done. If you want to create a tri-fold newsletter, Microsoft® Word® is not the only option. You might also want to try Lucidpress® or Adobe® InDesign. Sometimes one interface is easier for <u>YOU</u> to use than another. Choose the software package that works best for <u>YOU</u>.

Besides using the software that you find easiest to use, it is often a good idea to see the trends by industry in terms of tools being used by specific employers. I recommend looking at job boards online to view Instructional Designer positions and if there are any specific software packages mentioned. I have actually been turned down for a job because I used one software package over another. Said a different way, if companies in specific industries are using one simulation software, if those are the industries you want to become employed, you might consider looking at the software packages they use in-house and consider learning the latest versions.

Now onto the Named Packages. Each software has a different and specific usage.

NOTES:

_____

_____

_____

There are several tips and tables throughout this book!

Named Packages

Training Type	Software Examples
Classroom Presentation/Teleconference Materials	Microsoft® PowerPoint
Bound Chapter Book with Footnotes	Adobe® FrameMaker
Graphics, Logos, Icons, Buttons (all states) and Combination Marks	Adobe® Photoshop, Adobe® Photoshop Elements, Microsoft® Paint, Corel® PaintShop Pro
Software Simulations	Adobe® Captivate, Camtasia
Corporate Communications, Newsletters, Email Templates, Job Aids, Step-by-Steps	Microsoft® Word, Microsoft® Publisher
Computer-Based Training/Web-Based Training	Adobe® Flash, Adobe® Captivate, Camtasia
Complex, Branched Help Systems	Adobe® RoboHelp

Figure 1: Examples of software systems or applications that can be used for each type of training – these are only samples – there are lots more available.

As previously mentioned, there are often several options to create each type of training or training deliverable. In the previous table, you can see that the column on the left shows several training types and the column on the right lists the software packages by name. There are other software packages available for each type of deliverable – both FREE and paid options.

If you want to create a classroom presentation or teleconference materials, then Microsoft® PowerPoint allows you to create a slideshow with handouts based on the slide master designs and backgrounds that you select or create from scratch.

Adobe® FrameMaker is great if you want to create bound, chapter books complete with footnotes and pull quotes.

When it comes to graphics creation software, there is a multitude of options, from the simplicity of Microsoft® Paint® to raster graphics creation in Corel® PaintShop Pro to even a more complex suite complete with layering and basic animation in Adobe® Photoshop.

Now, let's say you want to simulate a step-by-step process in any software package, like how to create a mail merge in Microsoft® Word. If that is the case, the students may learn best by watching the mouse move for them on-screen while you go through the process for them. Some of the top software packages to accomplish this with audio or video might be Adobe® Captivate or Camtasia.

Next, if you want to create a corporate communication, quarterly newsletter based on sections/headers/footers, email templates, job aids or step-by-step procedures, then you could use Microsoft® Word or Microsoft® Publisher. Both of these options allow you to create your own creative designs or make use of the canned templates.

As for the computer-based or web-based training courses, there are options that will allow you to import Microsoft® PowerPoint® slides or include animated menus or even add in JavaScript. Some of these options include Adobe® Flash, Adobe® Captivate or Camtasia.

Finally, if you want to create a complex, branched help system (like what pops up when you click F1 on your keyboard while in many software packages), then Adobe® RoboHelp will help to create a seamless solution.

Purchasing software, especially if working independently, can be costly. You can search for trial versions or educational options, if you are a student.

Since we have taken a look at the Software, let's take a look at Non-Software.

Non-Software

Non-Software Tool	Examples
Microphone	Desk Stand: Blue® The Snowball Lapel: Sony®
Sound Proofing	Foam wall panels
Studio Space and Backdrops	Dedicated office space just for this type of work; could be in-home or a rented space
Lighting Stands and Light Bulbs	Might be formal stands or generic ones purchased from a hardware store; Use daylight bulbs
Camera – Video, Cell	Nikon® SLR, Canon® Rebel™
Camera Memory Cards	MicroSD Cards, small portable drives
External Hard Drives	Any manufacturer

***Figure 2:** Examples of non-software tools that may be needed – these are only samples – there are lots more available.*

Sometimes the company you work for will provide all the necessary software tools and accessories. Other times they will provide the items, but look to you for recommendations. In a few instances, you are totally on your own for the items in this table, when needed.

We already discussed the software packages that could be used for each type of training. Now let us talk to the non-software tools that *could* be needed in this type of position.

The first tool is a microphone. This will be really helpful, in fact, essential if creating any sort of audio or video. Never rely on the internal microphone built into your laptop or desktop computer. A desktop microphone will be helpful if sitting in a chair where users will not see your microphone – or you for that matter. If you will be creating video where you do not want the microphone to be as visible, then a lapel mic would be necessary.

Next, sound proofing. Sometimes, if the room you are recording does not have windows, you can get away without any padding of the walls or foam décor, but you will need to run some test audio files first to see what needs are to be met for your situation. Nearly every external sound gets picked up with a good microphone. One time when I was recording audio at home for one of my training course, my dog's dream sounds were picked up and I remember during playback that I had to rerecord what might have been an otherwise perfect recording.

The next few things shown in the table coincide with each other – that is – lighting, backdrops and bulbs. It is one thing to have a dedicated space, but it is also important to have good natural or daylight lighting and extra bulbs on hand. As for the backdrop, a good neutral black, white or grey tend to work the best – especially if the subject of your video has bright patterns.

Finally, you must have a good video camera with a decent lens. Nowadays, any DSLR camera and some smartphones may be sufficient.

TIP: Oftentimes video files are large in size. Therefore, invest in several memory cards and external flash drives. These flash drives could also be taken on-site when working with remote clients.

You now know that a lot of preparation and considerations can and should go into all the training you produce. If you have questions during the project lifecycle, it is good to know that several resources exist. Let's first focus on FREE resources.

_____

_____

_____

Resource Types

FREE Resources

In terms of Resource Types, you have several different options here to guide you in your quest to become a huge success in Instructional Design.

First, almost a lost art, the library. You can check out books, periodicals and perhaps even videos on just about any job from the library. People like myself donate books all the time after just the first read. It can be an economical means of learning about nearly every subject under the sun.

There are several companies online that offer <u>FREE</u> whitepapers or eBooks for you to come up to speed on a subject or even a company. TD.org has several resources available on that site. Several other companies have free Instructional Design resources as well.

Another option is to read about a successful Instructional Designer or someone that is already in the field, emulate their practices and study their habits, subscribe to their newsletters and send them email inquiries.

Finally, look up tutorials online and try to emulate that project with little to no guidance.

Next, we will view several paid resource options.

There are several resources available for a cost – sometimes a minimal cost to you. Here are several ideas:

- You could look into earning an Instructional Design certificate from your local, state or online university – this could differ from a degree program – both in terms of materials covered and cost.
- The Association for Talent Development or td.org has courses, books and certifications on gaming, evaluating the effectiveness of training and leadership.
- Student Guide's website or studentguide.org, has a listing of several tips and links about rapid learning and e-learning.
- You can always purchase a new or used book on sites like Amazon.com or really any retailer, buy a Kindle version for a cheaper price in an e-book version.

So now you know how to get help and online assistance. The next topic includes Training and Design Theories. We will touch upon to key methodologies or frameworks, including ADDIE and Scrum, beginning with the ADDIE Model.

So much to learn!
This is just the beginning!

Training and Design Theories
ADDIE Methodology
This is probably the most popular of training and delivery models. As you might have suspected, ADDIE stands for the following as an acronym:

- *Analyze*
- *Design*
- *Develop*
- *Implement*
- *Evaluate*

This methodology states that a Training Team or Training Developer starts by analyzing a project and the viability. He or She compares the project objectives with the objectives of the company or organization. If they are in alignment, then they move to creating an outline with objectives. Next, they turn the objectives into an actionable storyboard. This document gives the end-user an idea of what the end product *might* look like at the time of completion. The work is then carried out, the project is implemented and user feedback is sought after the implementation date. The users are encouraged to continue feedback.

The next topic shows a breakdown of the ADDIE phases.

ADDIE Phase Breakdown

PHASE	DETAIL
ANALYZE	The thought is that you start by taking a look at the business need, develop objectives and determine a roadmap for project completion on-time and in budget.
DESIGN	At this time, an Instructional Designer or Technical Writer will author the content of the training, regardless of delivery method, in a storyboard template.
DEVELOP	This is the phase in which one or more developers create the navigation, interactions, add in the instructional content and provide positive and negative pathing to give the average user choices.
IMPLEMENT	Upon successful completion of the timeline and training objectives, it is important to deploy the final training solution or end product.
EVALUATE	After you have deployed your training, it is important to monitor feedback, make changes to the content or interactions and stay involved with your students or stakeholders.

Figure 3: High-level overview of the ADDIE Model.

We will now provide a detail of each of the ADDIE phases.

Analyze:

The thought is that you start by taking a look at the business need, develop objectives and determine a roadmap for completing the project on-time and within budget. This often includes a training outline and the basis for the storyboard.

Design:

At this time, an Instructional Designer or Technical Writer will author the content of the training, regardless of delivery method, in a storyboard template.

Develop:

This is the phase in which one or more developers create the navigation, interactions, add in the instructional content and provide positive and negative pathing to give the average user choices. *For example, if the user wants to navigate a computer-based course through use of the Next button AND be able to skip around or back through topics for increased understanding.*

Implement:

Upon successful completion of the timeline and training objectives, it is important to deploy the final training solution or end product.

Evaluate:

After you have deployed your training, it is important to monitor feedback, make changes to the content or interactions and stay involved with your students or stakeholders.

You can always research the specifics online. This topic merely introduces you to the phases. The next methodology is known to be more of a framework.

Let's talk Scrum.

NOTES:

_____

_____

_____

Scrum Development

PHASES (5) OF SCRUM	INITIATE	PLAN & ESTIMATE	IMPLEMENT	REVIEW & RETROSPECT	RELEASE
PROCESSES (19)	Create Project Vision Statement	Create User Stories	Create Deliverable	Convene Scrum of Scrums	Ship Deliverables
	Identify Scrum Master and Stakeholders	Approve, Estimate and Commit User Stories	Conduct Daily Standup Meeting	Demonstrate & Validate Sprint	Retrospect Project
	Form Scrum Team	Create Tasks	Groom (Update) Prioritized Product Backlog	Retrospect Sprint	
	Develop Epics	Estimate Tasks			
	Create Prioritized Product Backlog	Create Sprint Backlog			
	Conduct Release Planning				

Figure 4: *High-level overview of the Scrum Framework Phases and Processes.*

*Training Models provide a guide
during the lifecycle
of the project!*

Another methodology in the work place is Scrum framework. Scrum is simply a framework for project delivery meant for projects with ever-changing requirements. Each scrum project consists of a Product Owner, Scrum Master and Scrum Team. The Product Owner is responsible for the vision, the Scrum Master acts as more of a team facilitator and the Scrum Team develops the project and completes the daily work.

There are several Scrum and Agile-related certifications available, including CSM or Certified Scrum Master and SAMC Scrum Agile Master Certification – both of these are available through a vendor called ScrumStudy. These are not the only exams, nor is this the only vendor of Scrum-related certifications.

ScrumStudy allows all exams to be proctored. That said, you must install Webex® and have a camera device so your exam can be monitored.

The project phases for this type of project include: Initiate, Plan and Estimate, Implement, Review and Retrospect and Release. As an Instructional Designer, it is not necessary to memories all the processes of the five phases, but to know that this is a popular methodology with Daily Standup Meetings for transparency to management and stakeholders alike.

The five phases will be detailed in the next topic.

NOTES:

_____

_____

_____

You are learning so much!

Scrum Phases

SCRUM PHASE	DETAIL
INITIATE	During this initial phase, the project vision and team are put into place for planning meetings.
PLAN & ESTIMATE	During this time, the team creates personas and user stories to aid in the development of each feature, and then, as a team, they estimate the work effort for each.
IMPLEMENT	This is where the team members meet daily with the Scrum Master for daily progress checks in what is called a Daily Standup Meeting.
REVIEW & RETROSPECT	During this phase of a project, the team takes a look at what worked and what was not as successful as expected in Retrospective Meetings.
RELEASE	Finally, the last phase, is for the shipping of deliverables to the end users or stakeholders. *TIP: Keep in mind that if you go for a Scrum or Agile certification, some are proctored and can be taken from home; whereas, other exams must be taken at a testing facility.*

Figure 5: *High-level overview of the Scrum Framework Phases.*

Let's take a look at each of the phases, starting with Initiate.

Initiate:

During this initial phase, the project vision and team are put into place for planning meetings.

Plan and Estimate:

During this time, the team creates personas and user stories to aid in the development of each feature, and then, as a team, they estimate the work effort for each.

Implement:

This is where the team members meet daily with the Scrum Master for daily progress checks in what is called a Daily Standup Meeting.

Review and Retrospect:

During this phase of a project, the team takes a look at what worked and what was not as successful as expected in Retrospective Meetings.

Release:

Finally, the last phase, is for the shipping of deliverables to the end users or stakeholders

TIP: *Keep in mind that if you go for a Scrum or Agile certification, some are proctored and can be taken from home; whereas, other exams must be taken at a testing facility.*

For the final topic, we will discuss Timing of Training – when employed and unemployed.

Timing of Training

Employed

IF YOU ARE CURRENTLY EMPLOYED, it can be a challenge to fit in training, to physically go and take a course or to even learn about something new on your own.

Sometimes your current employer will pay a specified amount of money annually towards furthering your education in a related field. This could include matching dollars or reimbursements. You might want to not only check if they will cover classes, but also study materials as well as professional memberships.

We discuss professional memberships in the USING SOCIAL MEDIA section.

What if you are currently unemployed? Let's talk about a few suggestions in this situation.

Unemployed

IF YOU ARE CURRENTLY UNEMPLOYED, you may be faced with the challenge of a lack of funds to start something new or difficulty in taking a different direction with your career. Times are hard, sometimes when you are faced with downtime, it may just be the perfect time to take a class on your own, obtain a certification and even update your resume.

Be sure to determine the Return on Investment or ROI when you are paying for education based on the cost to purchase.

Once YOU have been trained, continuing education is essential – some certified programs even require you to get PDUs or Personal Development Units to stay current on trends. Keeping up or maintaining a certification is much simpler and cost effective than initially obtaining the certification or training knowledge.

In the next section, we will detail Finding a Job.

Finding a Job

In January of 2017, I was laid off from my IT project management position. It was easy to lose hope. I would send off resumes almost daily into what often seemed as a black hole. I continued to send resumes out thinking that maybe just maybe it was because my ideal job just had not come up or become available.

I sent my resume to every recruiter in my local area, state and even any name I got ahold of throughout the country. That said, I turned my talents into money by creating animated courses for Udemy and writing books for Amazon. That is to say, I still continued my search months into the process, but wrote content as often and as long as I could every day. Over the weekends, I took time away for family and outings.

Sometimes you too may have to think outside the box. There are multiple ways to make money online from legitimate sources. Writing books and online materials is not only a way to use my degree in Graphic Design and Studio Arts, but also to do something that I enjoy – while feeling I am making a difference in educating students, regardless of location.

Now that you know a story from my life, let's look at the topics of this section. These topics include:

- Searches
- Keywords
- Job Hunt Avenues
- Resume Tips
- Job Boards.

Searches

If you want to find a job in ANY industry, you have to think like a hiring manager and know the skills, personality, certifications, experience, value and more. Each employer is looking for a different skill set and will write a totally different job description for the same job. Therefore, it is important to look at the current job listings across several industries in order to hone in on YOUR skills – to see what the market NEEDS.

GREAT job!

Next, search by keyword on job boards. That is, do NOT just search by the name of the title you are seeking, but also search for a certification name or job skill. In my case, I was searching for Project Manager jobs. Therefore, I made sure I searched for Project Manager, Six Sigma, Green Belt, Black Belt, Scrum, Agile and Scrum Master. I always counted the number of companies that required a PMP or CAPM certification and then studied in those areas.

Don't let the requirements scare you from applying. Perhaps an employer would like to have you on their team over a more qualified applicant because of your knowledge of a specific software application, based on a personal recommendation from a trusted source or they just really love your personality and willingness to learn. There is often a REQUIRED SKILLS area of a job description as well as a PREFERRED SKILLSETS section.

TIP: Be sure to apply even if you do not have all the required skills, as you never know who else is in the pool of available resources at that moment.

Next, onto Keywords.

Keywords

According to Google® Trends, the term Instructional Designer is a much more popular phrase in terms of the number of searches when compared to ILT (or Instructor Led Training). When searching for a job, you can use Google® Trends to see how often a word or phrase is searched for and in what country or region.

There are several terms that can search searched on or even used in Instructional Designer job ads. Several of these terms are as follows:

- *Training Specialist/Training Team Coordinator*
- *LMS Administrator or Learning Management System Admin*
- *Course Designer/Content Writer*
- *Learning Developer or Distance Learning Professional*
- *ILT or Instructor Led Trainer*
- *Learning & Design or L&D Associate*
- *Instructional & Systems Designer*
- *E-Learning or eLearning Designer/Writer*
- *Online Learning Professional*
- *Multi-Media Designer/Writer*

TIP: Don't underestimate the power of face-to-face networking too! You can sometimes know all the right keywords, but it may be more based on who you know than what you know.

Continuing on, let's visit the Job Hunt Avenues.

Job Hunt Avenues

When seeking employment, you need to determine the job title as well as the structure of the job you are seeking. *For example, would you be open to part-time hours, full-time hours, seasonal help, remote work, partially remote positions, FTE or full-time employee, contracting through an agency or consulting where you are typically project-based at a company but working for yourself.*

If working as a contractor or consultant, think of or research your going rate on both 1099 and W2. On W2, your taxes are paid. Whereas, on 1099, you are responsible for your own taxes, so your hourly rate should be higher. Dice is a website that can give you accurate figures for your current or targeted position within your geographical area.

When dealing with recruiters, it is best to get face-to-face. Always make sure that they have your most recent resume in case the perfect job becomes available at the last-minute with little time to fill the position. I have found success in creating my own, personal marketing packet. This 'packet' typically includes my latest resume, a summarizing cover letter, letter of recommendation and a business card. I ensured all copies were on slightly thicker resume paper. Remember, the key to any job or market is to stand out in a positive way. Some recruiters will know what your targeted position does on a day-to-day basis; whereas, others will not know or understand, even after you explain it to them.

TIP: A tip to keep in mind is that a good recruiter listens to your experiences and not only sends you probable matches, but also communicates each step of the way.

Have you ever attended a career fair or job fair? Perform an internet search. These are held quite often in your bigger cities and maybe held in a hotel lobby. Be sure to bring several copies of your resume and thank each person for their time. You might also consider having a small infomercial prepared about your past positions and experiences.

Word of mouth, as I mentioned before, can also be a powerful tool. One time I was at the gym and working out. In came a neighbor of mine through the front door. We got to talking and needless to say, I ended up sending him my resume and a small contract job resulted. You never know where your next job or position might result. It could come from a neighbor, like in my situation, or a former employer contact, professor, family member or friend.

There might be a Workforce Commission office near you that can assist with printing your resume and perhaps offering a critique of your resume and interview skills. Think of questions that a potential employer might ask. *For example, if they are looking for a designer with 7 years of experience, but you only have 5, highlight your positive aspects and recent accomplishments – that is – <u>TELL THEM WHY THEY SHOULD CHOOSE YOU</u>!*

TIP: *If you see a job posting, check to see if there is a personal contact or email address that you can reach out to on a more personal level.*

To gain resume tips, let's discuss a few bullets in the next topic.

Resume Tips

When you post your resume online, seemingly everyone on the planet (or so it would seem) can access the file. Therefore, <u>DO NOT</u> include any personal address information on the file. Before, you begin, layout the sections of content. Some of your sections *might* include: Summary, Leadership Skills, Professional Experience, Publications, Education, Certifications and more. Several recruiters are divided as to whether or not to include community service involvement.

Here are a few other pieces of advice from personal experience with regard to your resume that can actually translate to any job or position:

- Keep it simple – perhaps three to four pages, based on experience
- Use a well-formatted template or create your own
- Include a summary at the top
- Bulleted accomplishments seem to work best
- Highlight measureable numbers so they can gauge scope of work
- Always include where you worked as well as the location of the business
- Titles are as important as keywords

Job Boards

- Dice.com
- Ziprecruiter.com
- Monsterjobs.com
- Indeed.com
- Careerbuilder.com
- Beyond.com
- Linkedin.com
- Startwire.com
- Glassdoor.com
- Jobs.td.org
  (if a member)
- Theladders.com
  (if a member and seeking a higher income position)
- Managementjobs.com (if looking to manage a group of designers)
- Jobsforyou.com
- Jobsforme.com
- Jobsreport.com
- Linkup.com
- Jobs2careers.com
- Resumelibrary.com
- Jobcase.com
- Postjobfree.com
- Nicheboard.com
- Hirewire (although this option is not available to all areas

The previous bulleted items are *current* job boards as of this printing.

Be sure to list your resume on one or multiple sites. Also, ensure your resume is updated often so your name comes up at the top of the recent applications list.

TIP: *Some job boards allow you to receive emails when an employer has viewed your resume and even add a cover letter or other file – after-the-fact. Said differently, even after you applied to a position, you can generally see not only IF the employer or hiring manager viewed your profile, but sometimes how many times it was accessed.*

NOTES:

_____

_____

_____

Using Social Media

I recently became a published author and illustrator of a children's book about adoption. When you work for yourself or have a service to be rendered, you want as large of an audience as possible to buy into your product or service. In my case, I had never had a need to do my own advertising, as working in the corporate world, clients seemed to come to me instead of me seeking them out. That said, I worked with my publisher to not only design business cards and postcards, but I also turned to social networking sites to widen my marketing net and increase my customer base.

That said, as of this moment, I have three Facebook sites, one Twitter account, one Linkedin® profile, three YouTube® channels and a personal website with a blog. Sounds like a lot to keep up with, but each type of media or media avenue has a slightly (and possibly completely different) audience.

I have found that no matter which media outlet I use, I need to have a total branding – hopefully name recognition - as time goes on. You can do the same for yourself as well.

Professional Associations and Memberships

Let's take a look at Professional Memberships and Associations. There are several free and fee-based associations used for local, national and international networking. Here are a few named options:

- Linkedin® – did you know that you can not only create a job profile, but also search for jobs and add files for others to view and comment?
- TD.org (Talent Development) – formerly ASTD.org – paid membership to this organization gives you access to several online resources and discounted training and exams.
- Social Groups, such as Meetup.com – check your local area for a complete listing of local groups. Some of the groups are free and others come available for a fee.

Make an online presence for yourself – BE ACTIVE! In today's day and age, if you do not have some sort of media presence, your business is strictly limited to local word of mouth. That can limit the client base to only who you can see versus the country or entire world.

Create a YouTube® channel and monetize it – after you have the right number of followers and meet the NEW requirements. I have seen where people add hundreds of videos and still struggle to get the right number of views. The key, as always, is to tell people that you have a new channel. Make the content interesting. DO NOT just point-and-shoot a video without doing some type of editing, such as adding text and removing noise.

We will talk more about YouTube® in a bit, but first, let's look at Facebook® for a brief overview of several of the features.

Facebook®

Facebook® is the new MySpace® in the thoughts of many people. Facebook® allows you to create several groups or pages. It is wise to have a different Facebook® page for your personal work from your professional work. Additionally, you might consider having a different page per brand. In my case, I have a separate Facebook® for my family and friends that is my personal page, a unique page to advertise events and details related to my children's book and yet a third Facebook page for pageantry. Those are three different pages with very different types of content, feeds and sometimes different friends. Creating separate pages allows people to opt in to specific details about your life they may be interested in specifically.

Facebook® is really good at allowing you to add images, photos by album and video. Be aware that Facebook® does optimize for space to a lower resolution for on-screen usage. Another nice feature of Facebook® is the ability to create a page that is either personnel-focused or business-related.

If you are selling anything, you can pay to have an ad campaign sent via Facebook®.

As you build more friends or followers, you also have the option to opt into analytics.

As a part of my Udemy® course called, "Getting the Life of an Instructional Designer," I added a simulation on how to create a Facebook® group.

Now, onto Twitter®.

NOTES:

_____

_____

_____

Excellent progress to date!

Twitter®

Twitter® allows you the following capabilities:

- Create a profile with the ability to post daily or even several times a day
- Add a summarizing description and photo at the top of your profile
- Watch videos and live streams
- Have visibility into who is following you
- Private message a follower
- Follow any person or business that has a profile to see updates
- Search for content by name
- Include symbols like '@' and '#' with the same capabilities for tagging as in Facebook®

Next, let's take a brief look into LinkedIn®.

LinkedIn®

For seemingly decades of time, people used LinkedIn® as a networking site – and it still is used for that purpose. However, it is so much more than just a place to add your resume of positions held, certifications earned, community service completed and education.

You can even customize your link. That said, if you are giving out your LinkedIn® address, be sure to customize your link before you send the link. Additionally, you can see based on social level (e.g., 1st, 2nd and so forth), what each of your connections are up to and where they are working.

When you create a post, like Facebook®, you can see analytics.

Something you may or may not know about LinkedIn® is that you can search for jobs and contact the hiring manager, if their name is listed. In order to contact them directly through the job posting, you have to have a Premium account (as of this printing), but you could always simply search for a name AFTER viewing the post and connect with them. You might even offer to send them a resume, cover letter or letter of recommendation too.

As with most social media offerings, you can private message a connection (notice I called it a connection versus a friend).

If you want to teach people about a subject to drive traffic to your page, you might consider uploading a PowerPoint presentation using the SlideShare® option.

SlideShare®

By using SlideShare®, the power is in your hands to add previously-created content and presentations to 'drive' traffic to your LinkedIn® site. Again, if looking for a job, this can be a means of driving up traffic. Likewise, if you are advertising a product, this can be a free means of advertising or marketing. In my case, I use it to find freelance assignments and to advertise any initiatives I have going on at that time.

You could use it to teach students about a process as if you were a classroom trainer with a slide deck. Simply start by clicking Upload, and then loading your file. You will have to add a summarizing description and key Meta tag words.

This is a very simple interface to use. Within a matter of minutes, you can produce a link that can be added to any social media outlet. Just think of the possibilities it can do for you.

Next, we will profile another social site that is also very easy to navigate – YouTube.

YouTube®

Most of you already know what YouTube® is and may already have a channel. I have three separate channels. One of which I use to advertise my books as a writer and illustrator. On the second channel I include Tech Stuff, hence the name, and I include software demos, presentations and simulations. The third and final channel that I am starting is for product reviews. I think it is important to highlight businesses that I feel offer a great product.

Recently, YouTube® changed its focus to be on the number of views versus the number of followers – that is not to say that getting regular followers is not essential too. When you get people to follow you, they will be updated by the software that you have added a new video to your channel and are thousands of times more likely to view the new content.

Happy creating! It is fun and time-consuming to create and edit videos, but the finished product is often rewarding. In terms of my videos, I use a small Canon® video camera on a tripod. The camera itself was not expensive, around $200 at the point of sale. There are external lights with daylight bulbs in my studio along with different-colored backdrops.

For my editing software, I use Audacity for my straight audio files to improve quality. My videos are taken into VideoPad® Video Editor for optimal, clear output settings.

Next, we will look at Portfolios and showcasing your work online.

Online Portfolios

Let's take a look at Online Portfolios. There are several online options available for to you design your portfolio based on the level, if any, of interactions you want to have with your audience. *An example of a good portfolio site is wix.com. Several sites offer options, such as ecommerce, for you to sell products or services, proofing of content, invoicing, support, forms, email marketing and custom or template designs.*

Warnings

Let's take a look at Tips and Warnings! There are scam artists in every industry and aspect of life – even when searching for a job. If an email looks typeset, has a lot of special symbols and bad grammar, there is a good chance it is the art of a scam artist.

A scam artist may not be so easy to spot, sometimes they are people asking inappropriate questions to get into your personal information. Other times they want to sell you a product or service above retail; hoping that you will not research it out or notice.

Qualities of Great Training

One of the companies I worked for in the past had a corporate style guide that told all departments and all teams the exact placement of all logos, color schemes and fonts. When it came to graphics for both internally- and externally-facing publications, we even had a repository of graphics from which we could choose our images. Not every company has such tight guidelines.

The reason companies have such stringent guidelines is to keep consistency from team to team and sector or sector. The team I was a part of even had tighter processes in the form of a team-specific style guide. You might think that this limited our creativity, but in reality, it just took the guess work out and allowed us to spend time on technical issues instead of trying to find the best font.

Knowing what to expect allowed us to find answers to more complex problems and things that really mattered. In order for you to create great training, be sure you are spending your time on the right things. This section will help you by creating a checklist that may provide several suggestions to help you make YOUR training GREAT TRAINING!

NOTES:

_____

_____

_____

Way to progress in YOUR learning!

Instructional Design Checklist

CHECK	CHECKLIST ITEM
ANALYZE	
	Create basic flow outline
	Create course overview text
	Create project vision statement based on company vision statement
	Hold Project Kickoff with Management, Stakeholders and Team Members
	Schedule SME meetings to get functional requirements and business details
	Write course objectives
DESIGN	
	Check for consistency in terms of wording and proposed navigation
	Create storyboard complete with screen text, interactions and notes to the Developer
	Include the questions and answers for incremental and final quiz questions
	Know the audience that the training is intended
	Spellcheck content
	Use or create a Style Guide for writing
	Vary the training types offered to students (e.g., text slide, quiz options, practice exercise)
	Write strong course intro as well as summary
DEVELOP	
	All buttons are in the correct position, interactions and all states of the buttons are included (Up, Down and Over) - Next, Previous, Print, Audio, Pause, Menu, Exit
	All images have a caption or figure number
	Audio and video files have clear audio and visual presentation
	Audio has been created and published - perhaps with ability for user to turn on and off at the page- or slide-level
	Consistent colors, scheme and branding are employed
	Corporate branding, logo placement and fonts meet enterprise standards
	Course title and subtitles are clearly displayed
	Every page has a title or caption
	Hold incremental demos to SME and/or Management of the training to be offered, if time allows

CHECK	CHECKLIST ITEM
	Include a feedback mechanism for users to weigh in
	Page numbers are included
	Progress bar visible, if applicable
	Scoring for all quizzes is weighed with correct options and scoring %
	The Developer has clear direction in the storyboard
	The menu or alternative navigation has been tested and is available
	Use or create a Style Guide for design
IMPLEMENT	
	All the links are well-tested
	Course has bookmarking for users to leave and return to the same spot
	Course marks as complete or incomplete appropriately and was designed at the right size
	Develop for AICC/SCORM Compliancy to meet the requirements of the LMS or Learning Management System
	Final demo is a success with all incremental feedback incorporated
EVALUATE	
	Incorporate post-implementation feedback from user group

Figure 6: Sample Instructional Design Checklist.

NOTES:

_____

_____

_____

Nice job!

Be sure to take notes
as you go through the materials.

As you can see, I have included a sample Instructional Design Checklist full of items to ensure you can check off for your online, animated or instructional training. Not every item in the list will be applicable to your type of training, but it should serve as a comprehensive guide and maybe even provide you with an idea or two. My hope is that it will be a successful guide to aid you in giving the customer the most vast and comprehensive learning experience.

The checklist includes things to think about in each of the five ADDIE phases from outline and project plan to evaluation.

SME Interactions

When you deal with a Subject Matter Expert or SME, bear in mind that this person is not in that position to know every answer, but they will be able to guide you on what they might be looking for from a functional standpoint as well as provide you with business rules, background or even a history.

It is your job to ask the right questions with the right amount of detail. These are often busy people that expect you to know how to do your job and let them do theirs too. Said differently, it will be in your best interest to instill confidence on behalf of them for the work you do by being sure of your work, asking targeted questions and making the most of your time together.

I would also suggest that one of your questions be regarding how often to meet during the life of the project and who needs to be in those meetings – not just the frequency.

These thoughts, coupled by any other research you do on your own will set you up for success and contribute to your positive success as a writer or designer.

Now, continuing on to the next section by listing the Training Deliverables.

NOTES:

_____

_____

_____

Keep going!

Training Deliverables

Sometimes the client for which you are employed or completing work for may already have in mind the training deliverables that are needed. It could be that the stakeholder or client already has a training background and may have already done the research aspect of the project for you, all you may have to do is write or design. This is not often the case. A lot of the time, at least from my experience, you <u>MUST</u> know enough about how each type of deliverable is created, maybe have a template accordingly, and then based on that knowledge, make recommendations based on the scope or type of project being created.

For instance, if the employee base needs to be trained on a software package, a simulation or grouping of several simulations may be best. However, if a new and complex software package is being introduced to the market that is not like a previous package for the audience, then a blended learning approach may need to be presented and created. The computer-based training may consist of a menu system with navigation to several separate software simulations. Each might have a step-by-step guide. Each step-by-step guide may or may not then also have either a flow diagram, and/or, a business rules document that explains why the software functions as it does.

The same concepts can be applied to a non-software project. That is, the recommendations you make in terms of Training Deliverables would be based on the same knowledge from a training stand-point that you might use when talking about new Human Resources procedures and when presenting on soft skills.

Let's spend the new few topics discussing Training Deliverables. You will see an overview of each type to guide you in making <u>YOUR</u> recommendations to your client, users or stakeholders.

NOTES:

_____

_____

_____

You never know what you can do!

Types of Deliverables

This section will only have a few topics of detail, but will provide a wealth of knowledge.

Training Type	Deliverable Details
Classroom Presentation/Teleconference Materials	When presenting, it is a good idea to have a slideshow software with interactions to capture attention. **TIP:** *You might consider a remote control as your transition from slide-to-slide.*
Bound Chapter Book with Footnotes	As you know, certain software packages make footnote and variable reuse a breeze.
Graphics, Logos, Icons, Buttons (all states) and Combination Marks	As an Instructional Designer, it may not be your responsibility to create or know how to create graphics, but it can certainly make you a more marketable candidate.
Software Simulations	This is where you give the user the experience as if they are actually in the software. In this type of deliverable, the mouse moves as captions are being displayed.
Communications, Newsletters, Email Templates, Job Aids, Step-by-Steps	Each of these deliverables typically require that a template be created for consistency in a desktop publishing-type of software.
Computer-Based Training/Web-Based Training	Interactive training of this type might need to have a complex menu system, breadcrumbs, button interactions, alternative navigation, intro text and summary content and an eye-catching design.
Complex, Branched Help Systems	If you have ever clicked F1 in an enterprise-level application, you have seen an example of a help system – by where the user can navigate to related topics.

Figure 7: *Types of Training Deliverables.*

Looking at the table, you can clearly see that there are several ways to convey a message to a student base or to train them on a given topic.

Classroom Presentation/Teleconference Materials:

When presenting, it is a good idea to have a slideshow software with interactions to capture attention.

TIP: You might consider a remote control as your transition from slide-to-slide.

Bound Chapter Book with Footnotes:

As you know, certain software packages make footnote and variable reuse a breeze.

Graphics, Logos, Icons, Buttons (all states) and Combination Marks:

As an Instructional Designer, it may not be your responsibility to create or know how to create graphics, but it can certainly make you a more marketable candidate. Make sure that whether you are doing the graphical work or it is being outsourced, know the type of effort needed to create graphics at a high-level so you can make recommendations accordingly.

A combination mark combines text with an image in a logo. Icons can be important in software in terms of navigation.

Finally, buttons – these most often have an Up, Down and Over state so the user knows that the button is working and when they have moved the mouse over the image.

Software Simulations:

This is where you give the user the experience as if they are actually in the software. In this type of deliverable, the mouse moves as captions are being displayed.

Corporate Communications, Newsletters, Email Templates, Job Aids, Step-by-Steps:

Each of these deliverables typically require that a template be created for consistency in a desktop publishing-type of software. I once worked at a company that had a separate template for each of these that was strictly enforced in terms of usage. We even had version control and a document repository on SharePoint®.

The corporate communications tend to be used synonymously with release notes.

Newsletters typically tell about corporate initiatives.

Email templates can be used with any combination of attachments and show how an email should look like when the user first opens it to read the content.

Job Aids usually give business rules, charts or helpful details.

Step-by-Step documents are exactly what you might think according to the name – a sequential list of actions to be taken or procedures.

Computer-Based Training/Web-Based Training:

Interactive training of this type might need to have a complex menu system, breadcrumbs, button interactions, alternative navigation, intro text and summary content and an eye-catching design as we discussed.

Complex, Branched Help Systems:

If you have ever clicked F1 in an enterprise-level application, you have seen an example of a help system – by where the user can navigate to related topics.

NOTES:

_____

_____

_____

You are almost through the materials!

A Day in the Life

Dealing with deadlines can also be a challenge at times for an Instructional Designer. I recall a time when I was an independent consultant working for a client. We had incremental meetings by where I would get on-site after my full-time job and demo the progress made to date. The project was going well until they told me they wanted me to add in the ability for the audio on every page to be turned on or off at the user level by any user in any role.

That is, the scope of the project changed. My job was to get the project completed on-time and within budget. I knew enough about the training development side, since I was the Technical Writer, Instructional Designer, Graphic Designer and Training Developer in one. That said, I was able to quickly come up with a time estimation versus having to consult with a separate Training Developer. I was able to articulate to the client the number of extra hours and cost within a matter of minutes.

At that point, they were able to see the cost of the feature and decided to leave the audio as it was at that time. Said differently, they were able to come to a conclusion – one way or another – based on facts.

A huge part of an Instructional Designer's role is not just to learn, but to educate. Instructional Designers tend to be creative either in writing, designing or both. My advice to you is to learn as much as you can about the entire process so that you can speak eloquently to management and stakeholders and become a consistent resource. Customers will learn to depend on your knowledge and expertise. That is not to say that an Instructional Designer must have all the answers, but the more accurate answers you know – the better.

Let's talk about some of the qualifications and responsibilities that someone in this role could possess.

There are not only several qualifications that make someone a <u>GREAT</u> Instructional Designer, but also day-to-day responsibilities that can set the successful ones from the less successful persons. Let's first talk about qualifications that make someone a great Instructional Designer.

Qualifications

1. Possessing great communication skills when talking to all levels of the organization from admins to executives if the job calls for it at the time, is key. I recall a time at a previous employer, when I was walking out to my car in the parking garage on one of my first days on the job. I could not find my car in the parking garage, so I started talking to a man that I did not know, but knew he worked for the same company I did.

   We talked momentarily about our family and how long we'd been employed at the same place. As it turned out, he was the founder of the company, but I did not know that until after our conversation was well underway. The reason I tell you this story is that it is important to communicate well to everyone you meet and put your best foot forward. You could be talking to a founder or executive and not even know it until it is too late.

2. Handling conflicts confidently as they arise – they <u>WILL</u> arise – is also key! Sometimes the most difficult part of a job is dealing with different personalities.

3. Displaying excellent public speaking

4. Portraying the ability to have a successful work/life balance

5. Managing time – regardless of when things are slow or fast-paced. Here you will find a simple table illustrating time management and what a possible day in the life of an Instructional Designer *might* actually look like.

Day of Week	Detail
Monday	**Desk Time:** 8-10am – Sit with developers to 'knowledge share' **Meeting:** 10am-12pm – Talk about Requirements with the Business Team **Desk Time:** 1-3pm – Work on outline; 3-5pm - Storyboarding
Tuesday	**Desk Time:** 8am-12pm; 1-5pm - Storyboarding
Wednesday	**Desk Time:** 8am-12pm; 1-5pm - Storyboarding
Thursday	**Desk Time:** 8am-12pm; 1-5pm - Storyboarding
Friday	**Desk Time:** 8am-12pm – Storyboarding; 1-3pm – Work on system icons, create button states and author quiz questions **Meeting:** 3-5pm – Follow-Up with SME

Figure 8: An example of A Day in the Life of an Instructional Designer.

Notice there are several meetings with different groups of people.

Responsibilities

1. Determining the right training approach and deliverables – oftentimes the client will look to you for recommendations. If you state your case or give reasons why a certain type of deliverable is best, that might just be what it takes to create 'buy-in'
2. Creating a schedule, including milestones and deadlines
3. Interacting with SMEs and asking the right questions – this is something we touched on a bit earlier
4. Handling responsibly each of the review cycles
5. Knowing the types of reviewers and how to obtain objective feedback
6. Testing and troubleshooting your work or that of another associate
7. Publishing deliverables without error
8. Managing stakeholder and user feedback

Working for Yourself

I have worked for several large corporations that are household names as well as worked for my own business. When I worked in a corporate setting, many of my needs were met by my employer that meant I did not have to worry about them. Some of those worries included taxes, insurance, training and paid sick time and vacation time.

During the times when I focused on my own business, I found it a challenge to have a schedule. It took a while to be disciplined to a time clock when I had no meetings for a few days or anywhere to be. My life consisted of getting up and taking my child to school in my pajamas, sometimes to simply be an embarrassing mother.

Then, I would come home and write, animate and illustrate with few breaks until 2am. Sometimes working for yourself, you find yourself working longer than you did when you worked for someone else. The difference is that all the work is your work. You know that you maintain your lifestyle or not based on the work you put in and you ALWAYS get out what you put in to anything at any given moment.

The next topic shows several considerations and questions to ask yourself if working for yourself is the best option for YOU.

Considerations

When you make enough or have enough motivation to venture out on your own and work for yourself as an independent or small business, it can be both rewarding and stressful all at once. This is especially true when you are first getting started.

You likely have several tough decisions that I am going to point out from my background and let you decide if this is a right option for you. Working for yourself has a lot of risks, so you might need to get legal advisement first.

Then another major decision for you would be whether to obtain a DBA or Doing Business As or to start an LLC or Limited Liability Corporation with a bit more legal coverage.

NOTES:

_____

_____

_____

Here are a few MAJOR pointers if you want to work for you and get away from the corporate world, leave your commute behind you and work from <u>YOUR</u> space:

- What will you do for health, dental, vision or disability insurance?
- What will you do for life insurance? Keep in mind that many employers contribute to this point, but only while employed for them.
- How will you fund your retirement? Like life insurance, many companies also contribute to your retirement via matching dollars up to a certain percentage.
- Will you build in your own "paid" vacations once you have enough money saved up to cover the time away from your work? If so, where will you go? Will there be palm trees? Will it be a family destination? Imagine where you will go and work towards that destination as your goal. Ok, visualize this one.
- How will you stay up-to-date on the latest trends in your field? If there is a new software package on the market, will you afford it and learn it to your benefit?
- In what ways will you advertise your skills or services? Business Cards? Postcards? Newsletter? Blog? Vlog? Personal website? Social media? Word of mouth? Paid advertisement? TV? Radio? Newspaper ads? Perhaps you have the know-how to create your own personal marketing packet.
- Will you rent a space or work from your home?
- Will you have a partner? When should you hire employees?

This brings us to the end of the materials. I hope that you are now more informed as to the resources available, software packages that *can* be used, recognizing successful training and deliverables and how to BE an Instructional Designer – regardless of whether you work for a company or <u>YOURSELF</u>!

NOTES:

_____

_____

_____

You did it!

Summary

Congratulations making it through all the content of this book!

You have now learned about how to educate yourself, whether by going to a nearby college and getting a degree, obtaining a certification or by reading <u>LOTS</u> of <u>FREE</u> resources.

We also covered ways to handle search engines when searching for a job. It is never easy to land that first job, nor is it fun being unemployed. Searches are your 'friend!'

There are also many, almost endless ways to use social media to your advantage without spending a lot of hard-earned money.

I also discussed with you many qualities that make great training <u>GREAT TRAINING</u>! You now have a checklist of considerations – regardless of the training deliverable or type of learning to be deployed.

Then, you viewed a day in the life of an Instructional Designer in terms of qualities and responsibilities.

Finally, you were provided with several questions to be answered if you were to venture out on your own as an independent consultant and designer.

41524157R00024

Made in the USA
Middletown, DE
07 April 2019